Aah.. Adulthood

A Tug of War

Varsha Singh

BookLeaf
Publishing

India | USA | UK

Made with ❤ on the BookLeaf Publishing Platform

www.bookleafpub.in

www.bookleafpub.com

Dedication

To those whose hearts beat in rhythm with the world's
unspoken poetry, to the quiet souls who find beauty in
the fleeting moments, and to my family and friends,
whose love is the ink to my words.
This collection is for you.

Preface

Poetry for me is a place where the unspoken finds voice, where the moments between words can be as powerful as the words themselves. Being spiritually aligned since childhood, I have been able to notice the slightest shifts that occurred within and around me. This collection is an exploration of those moments-the spaces between breath and silence, joy and sorrow, the seen and the unseen.

In these poems, you will find fragments of my journey with each verse reflecting my thoughts, my resolve, and the secrets I've discovered along the way. Some of them are my quiet conversation with the cosmic energy that continuously creates, preserves and destroys. I hope that you'll feel the pulse of each word, each line, and find something within it that resonates with your own heart.

This book is not just a collection of poems; it is an invitation to pause and listen-to the world around you and to the voice within. Whether you are here for the rhythm, the story, or simply the quiet companionship of a poem, know that this book exists to remind you that even in our most solitary moments, we are never truly alone.

Thank you for holding these words in your hands. May they speak to you as they have spoken to me.

Acknowledgements

I would like to express my heartfelt gratitude to everyone who has supported and inspired me throughout the journey of writing this book. This collection would not have been possible without your encouragement, love, and belief in the power of words.

To my family, whose unwavering support has been my foundation—thank you for your patience and understanding during the quiet moments of reflection and the noisy times of doubt. Your presence in my life is the fuel for my creativity.

A special thanks to all those people who crossed my path whenever I prayed to the universe for supporting my life. Every time you showered your precious guidance and wisdom on me. Your expertise and insight have brought clarity in my life in ways I never imagined. Every conversation, every shared experience, has helped shape these poems.

To the readers, who make poetry meaningful: your willingness to engage with the written word, to find parts of yourselves in the pages of this book, is a gift I will never take for granted.

Lastly, to the quiet moments of solitude that allowed me to hear my own voice. The words on these pages are the result of the spaces in between- of listening, reflecting, and daring to dream.

1. I Am A Kid

I am a kid and, I live in you.
Life faces its highs and lows,
But it continues to flow.
With each trial, life grows.
O my friend!
I am a kid, and I live in you.
I bow down to those who
nurture me in their body-cage.
bringing me to full bloom,
irrespective of their age.

For many, I am a forgotten story,
Have been trampled in life's woe & worry.
Still, I am a kid, and I live in you.
Have more to see,
Have more to explore.
Have to win at the end,
That is for sure.
Yes, my friend!
I am a kid and, I live in you.

2. Mighty Self

Let's live with a bright smile,
Let no one snatch it from distant mile,
Move forward with soft power,
Develop the inner self like a tower.

Unshakable and indomitable,
The mighty self remains stable,
Amid those issues that revolve,
Nothing can waver its resolve.

3. Friendship (Not A Play)

How swiftly time passes.
Jokes, gossips & usual clashes.
Those were the days when we were great pals.
Now, between us anger and ego stand as walls.

Today, after so many years, sitting alone somewhere,
as I did my soul-searching, I saw you coming.
I opened my lips to greet you dear.
Hearing my raised heartbeat, I gave in to my fear.
I restraint, I fought within,
I hesitated, my heart sank-in.

I kept sitting, didn't even look at you.
Tried to pretend, as if I do not know you.
Kept my eyes down, with my throat chocked.
Allowed myself to keep my feelings locked.

I kept wondering, "Why can't I speak to my friend?
How can I let my anger, win at the end?".
Thinking, why couldn't you start conversation?

Focusing on you, I gave in to my reservation.

Pondering, what is in your mind,
Can we talk ones to finally find?
Asking the Lord to show me the way,
Our friendship was not a play.
Lots of questions in my heart,
Pricking like needle and dart.

We humans are slaves to weaker self,
Can something really help?
No freedom, no peace,
How should it finally cease?

Busy in finding each other's fault.
Why can't we just sit & talk?
Resolve the matter ones and for all,
Restore the friendship at one call.

4. Aligning Patiently

When I think of you,
Smile comes back to me.
Even in the darkest room,
I start to see.
Amid the rough autumn,
Flowers in heart bloom,
And I am out of my gloom.
Challenging daily to align,
Patiently growing strong yet divine.

When I feel dejected,
I think of you to get uplifted.
Inspired by you, day and night,
Can boldly take daily flight.
Thoughts of giving up goes away,
When you come along, throughout the way.
Your words vanish all fear,
Life becomes crystal clear.
Challenging daily to align,
Patiently growing strong yet divine.

5. Magical Dust

I Am Magic, I Am Miracle,
Unique And Special,
Box Of Creative Hassle,
Only They Can Tackle,
Energy Packet in Body Vessel.

I Am Magic, I Am Miracle,
A Speck of Divine's Dust,
Tossed To Remove Rust,
By Letting All Myth Burst.

An Unpredictable Mortal,
I Am Magic, I Am Miracle.

6. The Nudge

Little nudge is here,
What is then to fear.
Perfect timing O God!
I can fight the odd,
That nudge is here,
I can dare to dare.
Perfect entry O God!
You & I are pair.
Why should I then care?

Let me climb that hill,
My mind is still,
Stepping beyond the known,
Where the light is sown.
Looking up with awe,
Sight has no flaw.
That nudge is here,
What is then to fear.
I can dare to dare.

7. You & I

O My Friend!
I stay with you, I feed on you,
I get stronger through you.
I show the world, the worst side of you.
I remain hidden and, fight the good in you.
I stay with you, I feed on you,
I get stronger through you.

O Humans, you are awesome,
You live with me; you die with me.
Come what may, you do not betray me.
By remaining aloof, you let me bloom,
Don't worry, am with you in your gloom.
That's why I said,
I stay with you, I feed on you,
I get stronger through you.

O Dear! you prioritise me,
Thinking by your head, never by your heart.
When others leave you, I promise,

I will drive you in my cart.
O My Friend,
Although I have been the cause of your fall,
Since long ago, you & I have together stood tall,
And the world calls me EGO.
Thus, I say, I stay with you, I feed on you,
I get stronger through you.

8. Why Complain?

Easier is to complain,
Annoying is to take strain,
Holding ill-will is a quicker solution,
Instead, let's battle it with determination.

Joyful life is our goal,
Why take unnecessary toll?
As we play various roles,
Complaints can erode our souls.

No point in hating others,
Forgive whoever bothers.
Subtle is the working of mind,
Its peace, we must find.

9. Toleration

When confusion sprang-up,
It brought anxiety on the top.
Gave way to, highs and lows,
Thoughts wavered and agony arose.

Couldn't escape this situation,
Tried to practice toleration.
Holding grudges was no solution,
Only remedy was self-reformation.

Looking back, I feel assured,
Did not lose myself to temptation's lure.
Patiently, charting a way so true,
With each moment, my inner self grew.

10. Happiness

O Happiness!
You have always been with me,
Though invisible to my eyes,
But hidden deep in my heart.
I never knew this. I never knew this.

Though you seemed to drift away,
Like fleeting light at break of day.
Feeling you, I smiled at you,
Needlessly, tried to chase you.
You were so close to me,
I never knew this. I never knew this.

I promise to share and
spread your colour, far & wide.
May you touch yourselves,
In people's hearts and be their guide.

11. Shared Action

Another day of heavy heart
Just passed by,
Thinking about it, I feel shy,
Was blaming others for the pitfall,
As if I was "the best" overall.

Things happen through our shared action
Playing roles in our respective section
"All" includes me too,
Must not forget that basic clue.
Should have remained unshaken and aligned,
But another division left me confined.

Must act to overcome this regret,
Walk the path that is so great.
United with others in spirit
Must fight against my flip.
Finally, I have realized it.
Yes! I have realized it.

12. Cosmic Presence

When all odds rose up,
When no one stood up,
When faced with the flaw,
When thoughts were still raw,
Your smiling face touched me.

When no one was to be looked up,
When mind was hooked up,
When faced with reality,
When got shaken in totality,
Your beautiful heart touched me.

When confusion flared up,
When misunderstanding grew up,
When life was at whirlpool,
When heart acted as a fool,
Your lively words touched me.

How do you sense, how do you see,
The whispers that echo deep within me?

Though distant, still can feel,
Though invisible, still can meet.
This connection between us,
Over-rules all that fuss.
Will rise up against the odd,
Nothing can break this cord.

13. Long Distance

Neither sun nor moon can we embrace,
Yet their warmth, lighten our space.
Neither heaven nor lashes near,
Yet their presence we hold dear.
Neither far nor close we stay,
Yet in heart, we find our way.

Distance is but a fleeting guise,
Love endures with no compromise.
Effort we give, a bond we create,
With will and strength, we shape our fate.

14. Life, The Trainer

Grow through life,
Don't 'go through' life.
It's beautiful, It's huge.
It's energy, does prodigy.
Let's shine with each day,
Life isn't a play.

Grow through life,
Don't 'go through' life.
Not making our pretence,
an imitation of fake strength.

A duty calls, so vast and deep,
To touch the hearts of all who seek.
A goal so grand, both bold and bright,
To give our soul, to do what's right.

15. Smartest Fool

We get pulled down by our usual fears,
It brings nothing but tears.
Due to uncertainties of life,
It takes a turn in its rear.
Forgetting life's basic rule,
Acting as the smartest fool.
Extent of anxiety fills the mind,
Nothing works except negatives of all kind.

There is always a good hidden behind the trauma,
So, need the eye to put the comma.
Before the thoughts become reality,
Must perceive the truth in its actuality.
To live life of modesty, free of apology,
Must have a sound life-philosophy.

16. Parents

For parents we are still small,
though we can manage all.
They never let us fall,
Besides us in one call.

Their life revolves around us,
Ever ready to solve our lives' fuss.
With lots of love and care,
Sometimes biased, sometimes fair.

Taking care of every bit,
For their child must be a hit.
Lift our spirit in times of gloom,
Always praying for our rise and bloom.

17. Still Persists

That unseen bond, though unadorned, still exists,
That unregistered running thought, though unknown,
still exists,
I get puzzled, how come it persists.

That untold strength of relationship, though uncertain,
still exists,
That unstable mindset of dependency, though
unaccepted, still exists,
I laugh out; how come it persists.

That uncertain commitment of friendship, though
unsure, still exists,
That unabated trust, though unexpressed, still exists,
I keep wondering, how come it persists.

18. So What!

So what, if immunity is weak,
So what, if darkness plays its trick,
So what, if people try to prick,
Nothing can stop me, I'll carry on,
Nothing can beat me, I'll carry on.

So what, if fear steals my cool,
So what, if sadness over-rules,
So what, if problems try to fool,
Nothing can deter me, I'll carry on,
Nothing can defeat me, I'll carry on.

19. Gather Life

Planning fails sometimes in life,
Unfolds drama with great hype,
Blocks all wisdom to ponder,
Entangled in lives unique wonder.

Let me start with what is in hand.
Let me gather life and again stand.
Each setback forges my determination,
Victory is in next step, gives confirmation.

20. Some Connections

Amidst our daily struggles,
We build bond with others.
Few get lost and few crumbled,
Haunting us amid lives' juggles.

Confusing is this connection,
Easily visible in heart's reflection.
There's no commitment, no responsibility,
Yet forgetting them is no possibility.

Praying for their well-being,
To handle their lives' swing.
Without expecting anything in return,
May we meet at some road-turn.

21. Gift of Joy

Someone said,
Forgiveness is the greatest gift.
Others said,
It has the element of revenge in it.
Perplexed how to handle others' ill-will,
Good is fighting with the evil within.
Difficult to take this, Difficult to take this.

Learning the art of endurance,
Good must win through perseverance
In worrying about the life ahead,
The present must not get misled.
Shouldn't it be like this? Shouldn't it be like this?

Because, life unfolds after every comma,
Without any full-stop, it's an ongoing drama.
How can someone's view pull me back?
Have to gift joy to all, in a brand-new pack.
This is the way it should be. This is the way it should be.

22. Faithful Doubt

The road is straight,
Have faith in faith.
And doubt the doubt,
By removing its cloud.
Experience that joy,
Only faith, we must employ.
Have confidence to win,
Defeat is where we begin.

Vanquishing insecurity,
Standing up with purity.
Enjoy this voyage, embracing the light,
Don't begrudge, let dreams take flight.
Though journey is painful,
Just smile and be hopeful.
Victory awaits there,
Where fear has no layer.

23. Deep Within

Deep within something stopped,
That thought, just popped.

Accepting weakness is a task,
Heavy heart wears a mask.
Wanting things to move my way,
But fear doesn't go away.

Falling prey each time,
Still reviving to climb,
the summit of freedom,
Following the universal rhythm.

24. Start Afresh

Get up to grow up again.
Use the fall to stand tall.
Amid the typhoon.
Feel the monsoon.

Falling ground is good,
Use it as your food.
Give yourself a fresh start,
Towards the journey of heart.

Rocky is the path,
Joyous be the bath.
When totally resolved,
Life's puzzle will be solved.